Manx Cats

by Meredith Dash

www.abdopublishing.com

Published by Abdo Kids, a division of ABDO, P.O. Box 398166, Minneapolis, Minnesota 55439.

Printed in the United States of America, North Mankato, Minnesota.

052014

092014

 THIS BOOK CONTAINS
RECYCLED MATERIALS

Photo Credits: Alamy, Animal Photography, Corbis, Getty Images, Shutterstock, Thinkstock

Production Contributors: Teddy Borth, Jennie Forsberg, Grace Hansen

Design Contributors: Candice Keimig, Laura Rask, Dorothy Toth

Library of Congress Control Number: 2013952414

Cataloging-in-Publication Data

Dash, Meredith.

 Manx cats / Meredith Dash.

  p. cm. -- (Cats)

ISBN 978-1-62970-010-6 (lib. bdg.)

Includes bibliographical references and index.

1. Manx cats--Juvenile literature.   I. Title.

636.8--dc23

              2013952414

Table of Contents

Manx Cats

Manx cats are **special**. Most do not have tails. They are called "**rumpies**."

5

Some Manx cats have small tails. They are called "**rumpy risers**."

Manx cats have round heads.

They have large, round eyes.

The Manx usually has a short coat. It can be many different colors and **patterns**.

Manx cats have short, strong

legs. They are good jumpers!

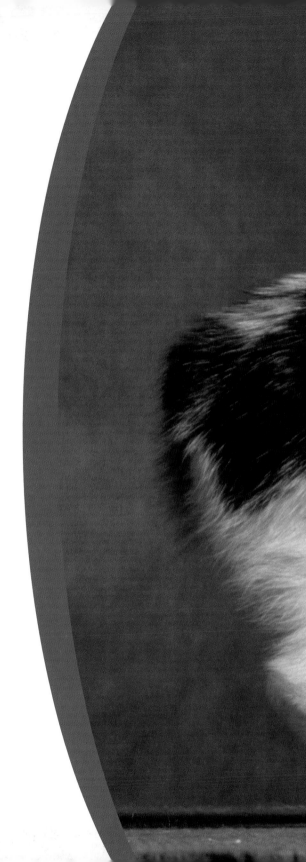

Manx cats are good hunters.

They easily find and catch mice.

15

Smart Cats

Like most cats, Manx
cats are smart. They
love to learn new tricks.

Personality

Manx cats like to play games.

They like to relax too.

19

Manx cats **enjoy** company.

They love their human families.

More Facts

- Manx cats were first discovered on the Isle of Man. That is an island in the Irish Sea.

- Manx cats are known to open cabinets and doors.

- Instead of meowing, the Manx cat often makes a chirping noise.

Glossary

enjoy – to find happiness in.

pattern – a regular marking.

rumpy – a Manx with no tail.

rumpy risers – a Manx with a very short tail. It looks like a nub.

special – not usual; unique.

Index

abdokids.com

Use this code to log on to abdokids.com and access crafts, games, videos and more!

Abdo Kids Code:
CMK0106